JUST RUN!

A complete guide to running a successful political campaign

JUST RUN!

A complete guide to running
a successful political campaign

By

Dale Fegel, Jr.

Dale Fegel Jr.

Published by Saranghay Studios
Foxboro, MA 02035

Visit us on the Web!
www.saranghaystudios.com
www.dalefegeljr.com

Cover by RL Sewell
Edited by Rachel Sewell

ISBN 978-0-9887068-5-9 (trade paperback)

*For Lauralee, my biggest fan
and always my First Lady!*

Contents

INTRODUCTION

R unning for elective office is a wonderful idea. Few endeavors will test your character and leave you a better person for the experience. Campaigning is one of those endeavors. It will test your mettle, reveal your character strengths, and expose your weaknesses. And, if you choose to do so, in the process, it will help you overcome those weaknesses and exploit those strengths.

These trials and benefits of campaigning are not limited to you, the candidate. Every campaign worker, paid or volunteer, and your citizenry, will also benefit from your candidacy. They will be better for having met you—an earnest, caring person who wants to do something to give back to the communities that have served you so well in the past.

Philosophically, the more candidates involved in the elective process, the better off the world would be. More issues would be discussed, more voters would participate, more relationships would be formed and only the best, most deserving issues and candidates would rise to the top of the democratic foam. Money and its influence on elections would be greatly diminished, as many candidates would divide the electorate and reduce its impact.

The ultimate success in any campaign is to win. This book will help you do that. But winning isn't everything and a successful campaign does not necessarily have to win. Winning comes down to one question: do you as a candidate best reflect the interests and ideologies of your district? The candidate who does will win that election.

This book will help you provide that reflection of your citizens without losing your own soul in the process.

To succeed, to the voters within your district, your campaign must present you both as you are now and as the leader you will become. It is a living organization. It is a start-up business that will last for only a short time. But, in the end, your campaign is about people. It is made up of people. People will be your greatest resource. They will make up the arms, the legs, and the heart of your campaign. The more people involved in your campaign, the bigger your organization and the greater the impact you will make in persuading others to vote for you.

There are no slick systems for winning elections. Campaigns mean meeting people and raising money. You can use tools to overcome certain deficits in the campaign—we will get to those later—but meeting people and asking for their votes is job number one and job number two is raising money to meet more people.

This book is written to the candidate, and, as such, I will be addressing "you" as if you were the candidate. That said, if you are not a candidate, but you are working for a candidate and you want to see him win, he needs all the help he can get. Armed with the information in this small book, you will be in a great position to give him the timely advice he needs.

WARNING! READ THIS BOOK ALL THE WAY THROUGH FIRST!

Many bumps and potholes await you along the campaign trail. Don't be caught unprepared. Read this book all the way through, then reread it for reference. You need everything in here. Don't fail needlessly. I kept this book short on purpose. You have only a few months to win your election. You need help now, and I'm here to give it to you.

Let's hit the road!

1.GETTING STARTED

As I stated in the Introduction, winning the election is how you, the candidate, best reflect the interests and ideologies of the people who vote in a certain district. It is important to start with a self-assessment. It is easy, and begins with the question, "Why do I want to run for office?"

The answer can be as simple as a total dislike for the current elected official or as complex as a concern about the treatment of animals at the town-sponsored shelter. Most political candidates fall somewhere in between: they don't like the current official and see an issue or two that needs to be addressed. You might not even have a gripe. You might simply be interested in running for office, and that works, too.

Whatever your reasons, it is important that YOU understand what those reasons are. Write down your answers to this question. You might need to refer to those answers to maintain focus on the real reason you are trying to get elected. This will be the start of your campaign journal; it can be written or it can be electronic. Either way, it is important that you KEEP a campaign journal. It can prove invaluable in this election and in future elections.

Once you know WHY you want to run for office, you next need to consider finances. Money is a huge part of any campaign and your campaign is no exception. Your finances WILL be a part of your campaign. How much money you will spend, and how you will spend it is up to you. You can depend completely on fundraising, contribute to your campaign, and loan your money to the campaign, or you could do all three. Yet, campaign financing will be your job as the candidate; as I mentioned in the Introduction, your number one job is to ask for votes and for money.

As a candidate you may have to file an income disclosure with the respective office that has election enforcement over the race for the seat you are interested in. Your town clerk, secretary of state, or state election commission are governing bodies that oversee elections. Be prepared to produce income tax information if required or requested. If you have financial issues that are yet to be remedied, such as out-standing taxes, pay them before running for office.

Check with your family first. This is an important step. DO NOT talk to friends or acquaintances about your plans to run without FIRST talking to your spouse and children about it. During campaigns, it is all too common to see candidates' families torn apart because they were unprepared for this important endeavor.

With the family in mind, if they disagree with your candidacy, don't run until they have resolved their opposition to it. Seeing a family member come out against you is one of the quickest ways to derail your campaign.

2. PERSONAL CONDUCT

During a campaign, morality plays a huge part of voter perception. Major indiscretions, and even the appearance of them throughout your campaign can steamroll your campaign and your image permanently. Plan how you will be seen in public and with whom. Also, you must guard whoever has personal access to you quite diligently. Turncoats, traitors, spies, and publicity hounds can infiltrate your campaign easily. Your inner circle of personal advisors must be people you can absolutely trust, including paid staff. If not, find a place for them away from you as politely as possible.

3. CAMPAIGN CALENDAR & JOURNAL

Keep a calendar of your campaign—start right away. This will be your personal campaign calendar, and then the campaign will have its own calendar, but it starts with your calendar. As you get them, start writing in all the important dates throughout the election year. Do not put this off. Deadlines are crucial: miss one and you will appear as blank space on the ballot. Jot down all of your dates for appointments with individuals, too. Keep a journal of your conversations and the subjects of meetings so you can refer back to it, if necessary. Your journal should include dates and times and who you spoke with during the meetings or phone conversations. You will not remember the content of all your meetings and conversations—nor will those with whom you speak. So, it is good to take notes.

You should be organized. This will make you an organized elected official. The problem with our political system is not spending, liberalism, conservatism, etc. It is disorganization. Politicians are horrifyingly personally disorganized. Be an organized candidate and elected official and you will do everyone a great favor. Do not just depend on a staff member to do this for you, because that greatly increases the chances of something or someone important being missed. If necessary, get help with from a trusted friend. If you are bad at it, become good at it. Being organized will make you an efficient, powerful candidate and elected official.

4. GOALS

Measure your progress. You do not need to know exactly the best numbers for each aspect of the campaign. Your upcoming research will help you fill in the blanks, though. Goals give you and your campaign direction. They will save you much stress and conflict. Some of your supporters will knock themselves out to meet your goals, which can be quite inspiring.

5. OPPOSITION RESEARCH

Once you have decided why you want to run for office and how you are going to raise money, and your family has given you the green light, it is time to do some research. The next question is, "How much do the voters of my district like this elected official, and care about the issues I am concerned about?" This question is a great wake-up call for what you are about to experience on the campaign. If the voters love the current elected official and don't care about your issues, you will face roadblocks. If they hate the incumbent, and agree with you on your issues, you could upset this official in the election.

How do you find out how the voters feel about the incumbent? The cheapest way to find out is to search your local newspapers online. You can conduct a survey and hire a professional firm to do it, which would be appropriate for a federal race or statewide race such as governor or U.S. president. Yet, even in those races, the newspapers do the work for you. Political writers spend time trying to write stories that sell their subscriptions. These journalists tear into elected officials' professional decisions and their private lives so the news is of interest to readers. After journalists have scoured politicians' lives, little information remains hidden. And, the same will go for you, too. In politics, journalism is a double-edged sword. The press can make you hero for a day and villain the next, and the villain stories sell better. So, let the press do your research.

You can also hire professionals to dig into the background of your opposition, through online vendors or investigators. This is good for private individuals who do not live under the spotlight.

One caveat about opposition research: do not fall into the trap of accepting rumors as facts. Your opposition might have lived sordid lives and you could be ready to attack them with it, but unless the source is credible, don't use the information, including online sources. Citing rumors as facts or using rumors to make tactical decisions in your campaign can steer your campaign off-trail. A credible source has a legal obligation to the information being given; such sources include law enforcement, journalists, attorneys, and government officials. If someone says, "Off the record, this happened to..," it is a sign of trouble. If you must endure the conversation politely, regard it as gossip and potentially damaging to you if you repeat it. Do not spout gossip during your campaign. And do not encourage your campaign supporters to spread it, either.

6. PERSONAL RESEARCH

Research yourself the way you researched your opposition. Find out what voters, the press, and your opposition can discover about you before they do. Then, have a response ready for your findings: good or bad. Start online with your name, phone number, and address. You can ask a trusted acquaintance to do it—he or she will tend to be more thorough. You can also hire a private investigator to dig more deeply into your past.

If you have had severe moral misconduct such as extramarital relationships, drug abuse including alcoholism, or criminal activity, record it for yourself and for your inner circle, even if it is not public knowledge. At some point in the campaign, you will need to address it if it comes to light. If the misconduct is public knowledge, you should come clean as you start your campaign, usually shortly after your formal announcement, but sometimes as part of your formal announcement. Do not think you will hide from your dirty deeds, even if you conducted them while you were a child. Campaigning is not a game of facts, but of perception. You must establish a relationship of acceptance with your potential constituents. As a candidate, you need to be fact-based to win a degree of trust to win votes, but in return, your constituents do not have to be fact-based at all.

7. SELLING YOURSELF

If you have read this far, you are sold on running for office. But, who else is sold on it? Your discovery of your opposition and yourself will go a long way to prove to those you need to support you to back your candidacy. Also, how much money you are personally willing to bring into the campaign is proof of how serious you are as a candidate. The less known you are to your constituents and to the party you belong to will require more of a personal financial injection. Until the votes are counted, money is the measurement of the health of a campaign and its candidate.

The most common response to the money and campaign health

factor is: "That is what is wrong with politics in the first place; politics should be about issues and debate of those issues. So, if the major parties are all about money, I should run as a third party candidate or as an independent." The unfortunate perception is money is the voters' and journalists' test of the overall strength of a campaign. "Who came first? The journalists or the voters?" can be debated forever. Yet, there is a way around the money issue.

8. TO PARTY OR NOT TO PARTY

The political system of elections is based on a two-party system, which includes the fairly new phenomena of nonpartisan municipal elections. There has been a huge effort to remove the influence of partisanship from elections. Campaigns today are candidate-driven, not party-driven, but voters want a candidate of one major party or the other. Nonpartisan elections still indirectly identify the candidates' party affiliations; if you are running in a nonpartisan election, the voters will find out if you are registered with a party.

Your best chance of success as a candidate is to pick a major party and run as a candidate for office under that party. There are two major parties in the U.S.: The Republican Party and The Democratic Party. All others are considered third parties. As a candidate, legally you do not have to declare a party at all in a partisan election and can still run for a specific office. This is called running undeclared, and the slang term for it is "independent." Yet, when people vote, they use party affiliation. Voters will review the candidates of the major parties first, then review the third party and independent candidates.

Most voters identify with a major party, even if they are not registered with that major party. Voters culturally define the major parties with specific keywords such as liberal, conservative, diplomatic, isolationist, socialist, or capitalistic. To voters, these keywords are descriptions and expectations of the political behavior characteristic of the major party candidates.

These keywords also define independent and third party candi-

15

dates, and voters will measure those candidates against these key-words or others they might invent. But, voters will always measure third party and independent candidates against the major parties they think the candidates are the most like. You will hear voters say, "I know he is a Libertarian but he sounds like a Republican." Or, "She says she belongs to the Green Party, but her platform is very Democratic."

This is where your Opposition Research becomes an important factor. Your research will provide you with the keywords and representative party affiliation voters want to see in their elected official. From that research, if you have not already, you should then best mirror the voters' desires and pick a party.

If your party selection is different than the voters you need to win, all is not lost. No candidate exactly matches voters' interests. The candidate who comes closest to those interests has the greatest success. Yet, third party and independent candidates have greater obstacles to overcome because most voters see themselves as members of one of the major parties.

If you choose a party, the next step is to find out from the party how party rules will affect your campaign so you can get on the general election ballot. Your state party should have a "campaign" kit that will give you the basic "do's" and "don'ts" of running for office. This kit should include the schedule for getting on the ballot. If you are running for a nonpartisan election such as a municipal election, the city or town clerk will have a similar packet of information. Legally, the state or town should provide specific information for the office you seek, so you, the candidate, are informed to resolve them of responsibility. It is important that you understand this information. If you miss a deadline or fail to plan your campaign calendar accordingly, you will be left off the ballot.

9 . CROSSROAD

This is a critical juncture in your candidacy. So far, your campaign is all preparation. At this point, if you want to continue, you have one of two choices: you can declare your candidacy or keep preparing.

By declaring your candidacy, you can start meeting the voters for the primary and start fundraising. This tactic works best for candidates who have no opponents, or for candidates who have ongoing relationships with political supporters from other interests in their lives.

More preparation is necessary for the candidate who has a primary or has not developed political alliances. If you have a primary in your party for the office you are seeking, then your Opposition Research starts over and will continue after you have declared your candidacy. Your Opposition Research should encompass the field of candidates competing against you in that primary. From your research you will get a sense of who the most competitive candidates are and which candidates to best prepare for. This research can often begin simultaneously with the Opposition Research on the elected official. Usually, you as a candidate will be informed of other interested individuals who want to become candidates.

10. POLITICAL ALLIANCES

Whether they support you or not, it is good form to introduce yourself to the people who will be politically involved in your candidacy. You should ask for their support even if you know they will never support you. The list should include paid and elected government officials, paid and volunteer party leaders, and individuals who have something to gain through your candidacy.

The best introduction is in-person. From your conversation, you can then gauge how much they support your candidacy. Always end by asking for their support, even if it is a generic request. After every meeting, record your thoughts in your campaign journal.

Do not expect to be greeted warmly and included in the club of politics. Also, do not discount the individual for his or her lack of fanfare for your candidacy. That individual could end up being an ally. You do not know what the future holds, and with that, barring criminal activity, you should welcome others as much as possible.

Handle people with a criminal past or suspected criminal past cautiously. Even if you do not know it, your personal conduct is closely observed (see PERSONAL CONDUCT). Your opponents' best weapon is to destroy your character, and they will do just that. So, do not make it easy for them to derail your candidacy. If it does not feel or look right, just do not do it. You can have a successful campaign and be legal and legitimate while you maintain your integrity. Participating in criminal activity to improve your candidacy, even if you are not aware of it, is unnecessary and wrong. Be aware and be prepared.

11. TREASURER

As you, the candidate, conduct your various research, your treasurer should study the rules for reporting your contributions and expenses. Regardless of the size of the election you are part of, there is a large body of information to digest. At least once a week, keep in touch with your treasurer's progress.

12. FUNDRAISING RESEARCH

As you converse with political leadership about your candidacy, names of financially prominent people will start to surface who have contributed to candidates in the past. These names are a good source of information. You should list them in your journal. These individuals will also provide names of other potential contributors who could be sympathetic to your candidacy.

If other candidates have challenged your opponent in past elections, their fundraising records of contributors will be a vital resource in soliciting more contributions. You can find these records with the government office that oversees your election, or you can ask the former candidates if you can use their lists.

Make a list of your potential donors. This list can start with friends and family. Then, it should include those donors who can make the greatest contributions down to those who can make the least.

13.WEB PRESENCE

You should have an idea of what you want your web design to look like. Your website should include the basic format: Biography, Issues/Events, Donations, Volunteers. These four categories are the easiest and most effective for your supporters to use.

14.PUBLIC SPEAKING

Candidates are public speakers. For most people, public speaking can be frightening. The best way to overcome your fear of public speaking is through the age-old strategy of practicing in front of a mirror, which still works well. About 10 times daily, repeat your answer to "Why do you want to run for office?" As you become comfortable with giving yourself these answers, begin to ask yourself questions others might ask you.

The best way to practice speaking in public is to videotape yourself giving a speech. It will help you fine-tune your presentation. You will observe nervous mannerisms and filler words. Begin to eliminate these from your presentation. It can be awkward and uncomfortable. Yet, within a short period of time you can polish your presentation and give a clear and concise speech.

15.GOOD TO GO

For the greatest chance of success, you would begin your research about two years before your general election. This would give you a solid year of research and laying the fundraising foundation. Then, a year from the general election you would declare your candidacy and begin to ask for votes and for money.

Many candidates want to just jump in regardless of party or plan, though. The reality is, your campaign will end up trying to accomplish the aforementioned instruction during the campaign anyway, which can add a lot of stress.

But, you are still unswayed. You want to cut to the chase. Then go ahead, as long as your treasurer is ready to join the campaign.

16. ANNOUNCING YOUR CANDIDACY

The minimum requirement for declaring your candidacy is a treasurer, someone other than yourself, the candidate. You, the candidate, will sign the declaration for candidacy with the appropriate government entity such as your state election commission, secretary of state, or town clerk. The treasurer will also sign. Once this is done and submitted, you are now an official candidate for your respective election.

The voters see this declaration in the form of a formal announcement. Voters do not usually know about the legal process of declaring your candidacy. Voters are used to presidential candidates holding their formal announcements on TV. Yet, most other elections and their candidates are more likely to make formal announcements with a press release.

As soon as you sign your papers to declare your candidacy, the press is magically notified. So, it is best to have your formal announcement written as a press release, or schedule the event and then invite the press after you sign your declaration.

There is no best way to formally announce your candidacy. It is really a matter of preference. A fundraising dinner with a formal announcement and a popular political keynote speaker can be a fun and exciting way to announce, but a lot of work. A press release makes your message easy to misinterpret. Even if you do nothing but sign your candidacy papers, more than likely the press will call you and ask you questions about your candidacy.

The simplest way, again, is the press release formal announcement. It is easy to research on the Internet what a press release should include. Follow the format; it is best to include a brief biography, no more than three issues, and an appeal for support, along with your web address. Send this release to newspapers, radio stations, and TV stations that cover your district. Over the following few days, try to follow those news outlets and see what they say. If one of the outlets fails to talk about your candidacy, call them and see if they will.

17.WORKING WITH THE PRESS

Always be polite with the press regardless of how prying or disinterested they can be. A candidate can easily fall into the trap of taking the questions and attitude they perceive of a reporter personally. The bottomline: the press needs news to sell advertising. That is it! Your contribution as a candidate is just that—a contribution. When you speak to the press or give them a press release, you are giving them a free contribution so they can sell advertising. It is a business transaction. You can say nothing to them or you can say everything. And the press has the right to choose whether to promote your free contribution.

Answer the reporter in a clear. fact-based manner. As a new candidate, it is best to get the questions in writing and to answer them in writing, so there is little misinterpretation. Add some emotion to your answers, but ensure the emotion is right for the issues. The press is not your ally and they are not your enemy; they are a hammer in your political tool box.

The press is not the best way to get your message to your district. It is one way, but it is compromised because the reporter has the ability to change your message. This irritates a lot of candidates. Candidates often feel misquoted or misrepresented. Remember, politics has a lot to do with perception. And the voters' perception of the press or the reporter or the company the reporter works for can be suspect. So, when they misquote you, do not fire back at the reporter or the press in general for sloppy journalism; see it as a chance to further define your message so it is easier to understand the next time you offer it.

18. CONTROL THE MESSAGE

You, the candidate, have complete control over what you want voters to see, hear, and feel about you and your campaign. Once you allow another person such as the press, a spokesperson, an endorsement, etc., to frame your message, you have lost control. The only one selling your candidacy should be you, the candidate. Your campaign is simply a personal appeal to the voters that you are the right person to represent them. There are no tricks, gimmicks, and slick answers around selling yourself to the voters directly. It is the most effective way to campaign, whether you are a first-timer or an incumbent.

If your opponent, the press, and your ex-spouse all gang up and tell the world what a terrible person you are, that is not losing control of the message. You cannot control what everyone is going to say about you. But, it is losing control of the message if you do not reinforce what a great elected official you are or will be. What losing control of the message is, is to let another person sell you to voters, good or bad. Give the voters a fair chance to choose whom to believe. Speak up for yourself that you are the right person to represent them.

Personal attacks will come, and sometimes it will feel as if everything around you is under fire. It is the normal process of a campaign. And, even if you are the best person to ever walk the planet, someone will find something less than nice about you and reveal it. It can sting, but keep the course, stay on message, and sell yourself as the right person to represent the people.

19. BEING PRESIDENTIAL

An interesting phenomena takes place in voters' minds when they choose a candidate. They compare that candidate to the President of the United States, regardless of the office the candidate is running for. So, it is prudent to appear as presidential as possible at all times. To be a successful choice in the voters' minds, a lot of looking, speaking, and acting the part is involved.

Is this fair? Certainly not, unless you are running for president. But, it is a reality you, as the candidate, will face. And, the sooner you resolve to accept appearing presidential, the easier your campaign life will become.

Think about how you would want the president to address you personally. How would you like the president to handle your concerns? You probably want to improve how the president comes across. Your voters feel the same way. As a candidate you have the opportunity to look, speak, and act the way you would want the president to look, speak, and act.

Looking presidential is important in how you deliver your message. Every piece of literature, private conversation with a donor, interview with the press, speech, or advertisement you broadcast should be consistent with appearing as presidential as possible.

20. BRANDING YOURSELF

As you look, speak, and act presidential in the course of your days on the campaign trail, you will begin to brand yourself. A voter is a consumer of political products. In a simplistic way, you as the candidate are the political product. To purchase you with their vote or contribution, the voter wants to see the presidential packaging, and also consistent, stylish rhetoric.

You and your campaign will be successfully branded when you meet voters on the street and they can tell you who you are, which office you are running for, your party affiliation, and what your issues are. This comes from repeatedly telling people who you are, why you are running, and asking for their votes, shrink-wrapped in a presidential package.

21 . TONE

I f your candidacy is a color, what would it be? Would it be red, blue, green, white? Color can greatly display the emotional tone of your campaign, and symbolize your approach to your world of politics. Do you want to be fire engine red, revealing outward frustration, aggression, or a call for action? Or, as green as grass, showing concern for others and the world we live in?

The tone of your campaign will be a rainbow of color. One issue you will approach with fire red urgency, another with cold, calculated, uncompromising blue, or another with the purity of white. To look presidential is to give an issue the right emphasis, color, and emotion. If you are one color all the time, no matter the issue, voters will misinterpret you as too angry, too cold, or too sensitive.

The best way to lead your message is with a biography that shows a warm color of caring; then your first issue will be one of fiery red— an "it must be stopped now" sense of urgency. Your next issue will, in contrast, be blue for an uncompromising standard of behavior. And, the last issue will again be a warm color: sensitive to the community or to the environment.

BEWARE ! !

Many candidates will maintain a neutral or "above the fray" tone during the course of their campaigns in order to be perceived as unflappable to the negatives that will be discharged against them and the negative tone their campaigns will unleash on their opponents. So, the candidates never attack their opponents, but a spokesperson on their campaigns does. The effectiveness of such a popular strategy has never been determined; some seem to win with it and some do not. Yet, seemingly savvy party activists and donors often promote first-time candidates using this strategy. Hawking such a strategy, first-time candidates can feel intimidated or like they owe some allegiance to their new supporters, and try to spew negativity, causing them confusion and a loss of control of their message.

Refrain from letting another person speak for you. You are selling yourself to the voter. It is a personal relationship. If you attack your opponent, you do the attacking. It is your message, so maintain control and maintain the correct tone.

22 . MESSAGE

Your message is what you want the voter to know about you and your candidacy. It is not just a slogan or a theme, it is the rhetoric, emotion, and the theater your campaign portrays. Everything with your name on it should be consistent with your message, from the decorations in the office and the fundraising phone calls to the bumper stickers. A volunteer who wears your button defines you as much as the popular politician who endorses your candidacy.

Your message is the most critical ingredient in your campaign. And, to most first-time candidates it is the most neglected ingredient. The shoot-from-the-hip-cowboy candidate will eventually make a ghastly, costly mistake that will ruin his or her candidacy, if not his or her complete political reputation. As a candidate, you are better off saying less than more, reacting less than more, and including less than more.

Remember the best chance of winning is to reflect the interests of the voters in your district. Your message needs to reflect their interests as they marry themselves to your interests as a candidate. From your research, you will find the interests voters take to heart. If you share similar interests, use them in your message. Let the push pieces, stickers, yard signs, TV advertising, office staff, speeches, or your apparel reflect those interests. Through your message, the voter should feel a connection to you.

Candidates will pander to voters to gain support, meaning they will be phony in their support of voters' interests, hoping voters will believe they are genuine. There is no need to pander, to be phony about anything. Your message should consist of the interests you and the voters agree on. You will not agree on everything. So, focus on the ones you do and emphasize the ones your opponent is forgetting about.

As you travel your district, pay attention to the mundane characteristics of your voters. See where they live, what they drive, how they eat, what they wear, or where they work, and think of how similar you are to them. Then ask yourself, "Do I have anything in common with them? And if I do, does my campaign reflect those common interests?" As the campaign rolls on, continue to ask yourself these questions so you will maintain the focus of your message.

Candidates will often take photos, choose colors, or select bumper sticker font sizes out of personal preference, rather than to appeal to voters. Some of it is ego; some of it is political ignorance. Your campaign will be successful as the voters understand you to be a benevolent political servant. Your message should fulfill voters' desires. Choose what your campaign displays through thinking like the voter first.

23. OFF TRACK

There will be times during the campaign when, in one form or another, your message is compromised. Whatever causes the problem, remove it fast. A person or an advertisement, or both could compromise your message. Again, get rid of them quickly. Campaigns are not the appropriate setting for rehabilitation or education. People and ideas that are at odds with your candidacy do not belong in your campaign. You must maintain control and show the leadership necessary to maintain control. It can get messy, but get rid of them—legally.

24. GET OUT YOUR MESSAGE

Your message begins with you. Look in the mirror. Are you groomed the way you want the voters to see you? Your hair, nails, teeth, complexion, and body image should all be in-line with your voters' expectations. Maintain your hygiene. It shows the voters respect, and that they count.

Smile! Practice smiling all the time. Give your voters a firm handshake and a smile, even when you are ready to fall down with exhaustion. It is no secret that people like to be liked. A smile will help voters warm up to you.

Your clothes should also match voters' expectations. When it comes to clothes, the worst thing you can do when meeting voters is to under dress. A casual approach to your attire can kill your campaign. The voter can dismiss you without bothering to hear a word. Do not be sloppy in your appearance.

Keep your promises. If you say you will call a donor at a specific time, keep the time. If you say you will look into an issue for a voter, do it. If you can't or don't want to, do not promise it. Your message includes your actions. You will lose trust instantly if you do not follow through with what you say you will do. This is where less is more, say less, and commit less, will prove to be more in the end. It is easy to try to be all things to all people, but that is not why you are running for office.

BEWARE!!

You are running for office on a specific platform and a strong element of popularity. Don't complicate this process by trying to solve the world's problems. If a voter or donor requests special attention to a specific issue that does not match your message, it is a trap. Stay the course and stay on message. If you decide to accept the request, make sure it is something you and the campaign can deliver. Save special requests for after the election when you can actually try to do something, but even then it is no guarantee. There are many political mountains to climb, but you can climb only one at a time, so be prudent in your commitments. Do not be afraid to tailor the request back to your message.

For example, you can save yourself a lot of time and trouble by telling the voter, donor, or volunteer, "That is a very important point. Yet, what is before us is an insurmountable deficit that requires immediate action. Our town is going broke. Can you help me with this so we can get to your issue?" Set the priority and ask for their help.

First-time candidates think the message is the platform. But, that is just part of it. The platform is just that—a foundation from which to build from. Again, voters are looking for the presidential package. They want the look, the talk, and the charisma embodied in the message.

It is important for you to have a handle on your message because the first time you are going to take this message out for a walk is when you collect your signatures to get on the ballot. This is your introduction to the voter. And they are going to ask questions and look you up and down. This is the part of the campaign called The Petition.

25. PETITION

After you declare yourself a candidate, you are not on the ballot until your petitions have the correct amount of certified signatures. There is a nearly nine-month timeframe before the general election for your office that petitions must be filed for your candidacy; the petitions can also be called nomination papers. Each office requires a certain amount of certified signatures of registered voters within your declared party who want you on the ballot.

Typically, you, the candidate, and some supporters will meet voters at malls, stores, post offices, or homes to collect their signatures. Depending on the size of your district, it is important to make sure you sign all the petition forms, and the voters' signatures and addresses are legible so the certifying agent can read them easily and not contest them or throw them out altogether. For an elected office with a large district, because of the large number of signatures required, the campaign might need to hire people to collect signatures.

There is a start date when these petitions can be "pulled," along with a deadline for submitting them to the respective town or city clerk for one round of certifying, and then the secretary of state's office for the last round of certifying. Once the last round of certifying is done and your effort has been successful in surpassing the threshold amount of certified signatures, you, the candidate, appear on the ballot. You will be on the primary ballot for a partisan election, and if you run undeclared, for the general election.

Collecting signatures is a chance to meet voters and get to know them in a democratic way, but it takes time. Voters will sign your petition because they just believe in the process. It is a great time to present the voter with a "push piece," a card or letter that outlines your candidacy.

The push piece should be in a color and size that is common or popular for your district and in-line with your message. To increase name identification or name i.d., it helps if it features your photo. The physical act of taking a push piece from you then looking over your photo and the message on the piece goes a long way for the voter to not only remember you but also to begin that relationship of trust enough to vote for you.

26. FUNDRAISING

Petitioning is important. If you fail to get certified to appear on the ballot, your campaign is over!

If the office you are running for is at the state senate or county commissioner level or lower, it is best to get the petitions certified first, before fundraising. If the office you are seeking is higher, such as governor or U.S. representative, you will need to do some fundraising before the petition process begins; the large district campaigns at this level often require professionals to administer the petitions and see them through certification, with a cost per certified signature. A statewide office up for election such as governor often requires 10,000 certified signatures to make the ballot, which means about 13,000 signatures would need to be collected. An amount this size is usually too much for the candidate and for volunteers to do themselves.

Fundraising is distinctly different than campaigning. Fundraising is the lifeblood of a campaign. And, it is the hardest part of the campaign. For most candidates, asking people for money is much harder than asking them for votes.

Contributions come with a string attached. That string is DIRECT ACCESS. No matter the amount of the contribution, the donor wants some level of access to you, the candidate, your campaign, and you, the elected official. Every donor would love direct access to you for only a dollar, but that is not reasonable. That is where you as the candidate need to set the limit on the amount of the contribution that will bring them direct access to you.

There is no fundraising template that works well for all campaigns. Large district campaigns will have certain professionals in charge of specific types of fundraising. Smaller district campaigns will rely on the candidate for the bulk of the fundraising. Fundraising falls into four distinct categories: phone calls, dinners, letters, and websites.

27. PHONE CALL FUNDRAISING

Phone call fundraising is also appointment fundraising. Through your research you have identified donors you think are sympathetic to your campaign and can afford to contribute the maximum amount allowed. You would contact prospective donors through letters of quality rhetoric, paper, and letterhead. These letters would include a brief background, issues important to the donor, and an invitation to contribute after a brief meeting. To set-up the appointment, a phone call is made after the letter has been received. During the appointment, you would offer an invitation to contribute the maximum amount allowed. If you have not done this kind of fundraising before, it can be quite intimidating.

This type of fundraising is the most time consuming for you, the candidate, and the bulk of what you will be spending your time on during the campaign. It is also the most abandoned type of fundraising when a candidate gets the chance.

The reason is the candidate is not converted to their own candidacy. One of the hallmarks of a successful candidate is their almost preacher-style politics. They are converted to their cause. They believe and trust themselves, they will fear and risk rejection to accomplish what they know is right. That means they will ask people with the means to contribute the maximum to their campaign.

A small number of people will contribute the most money to your campaign. These people will want a great degree of direct access to you as a candidate and as an elected official. They will remain loyal to you as you remain loyal to them. These donors will want to be able to influence your political direction and you should listen to them, only if they agree to contribute or have contributed to your campaign. Do not waste your time with people who want to tell you what to do, and then wait to see if they will give you a check if you do what they ask. Contributors know that you might not win, but they need you to further their agendas and that usually is tied to their monetary gain. Your research should have made you aware of the selling point of your message to these contributors. They need you to get more of what they want. Somehow government stands in the way. You then connect those two worlds and they pay to be involved, and its starts with your candidacy.

28.DINNER FUNDRAISING

Dinner fundraising is an expensive, time consuming endeavor with mediocre returns. Candidates of large district campaigns will hire a professional to manage these fundraisers. These dinners are not just for fundraising, but for organizing volunteers and getting press coverage. The donors pay well over the cost of the meal, with the difference going to the candidate as a contribution.

This type of fundraising will be popular with supporters, party leadership, and volunteers. Dinners are a good way to add fun to the campaign, and to recognize key donors and contributors and to thank them for their support. Your list of contributors who have paid the maximum contribution amount would get in free.

Dinners can be as high-end or as low-end as you want. Different districts are accustomed to certain expectations. A backyard barbecue may be appropriate for one district, but totally insulting to another district that expects catering and linen. Again, dinners should reflect your message and reinforce it to those who attend.

The invitation and attire should be as formal as the setting where the dinner will take place. The more formal the setting, the more formal the invitation and attire. Yet, for those you wish to attend, all events should follow-up with a phone call as a reminder.

BEWARE!!

Dinner fundraising is a preferred choice of supporters and party leadership for another reason, too; they want a meal, to be recognized, and a place where they can socialize. Do not schedule too many dinners from their advice. Keep dinner events to a minimum. They have their place, but if too frequent, can be incredibly distracting to the candidate and the campaign.

29. LETTER FUNDRAISING

Every election cycle, you probably get a card in the mail from a candidate asking you to contribute to his or her campaign, for a good reason. The best way to warm up like-minded voters and cover the cost of the printing and mailing is to send your push piece as a postcard fundraiser. This introduces the candidate, you, in a tangible way to those who would most likely vote for you. But they will not vote for you if they do not hear from you. The letter or postcard clears this hurdle.

Attach a special note to those voters you identified from your re-search who have given to other candidates in the past, with at least a handwritten signature, and politely ask them to give to your campaign. The other voters should receive a postcard asking for their contributions.

The postcard should be similar to the push piece, but it needs to comply with appropriate election laws. You and your treasurer should ensure the printing of the postcards or letters are compliant before you pay the vendor.

The contributions will begin to come in from the mailing. If only a few contributions come back, do not be depressed. A good monetary return will cover the cost of the printing and the mailing—that is all you are aiming for. You will then take the list of these contributors and hit them up again for more contributions or fundraising dinner invitations in subsequent mailings.

TIP!!

To get a better monetary return from your mailings, give contributors amount options. Ask for the maximum amount. But, then give lower amount options. People feel important and surprised you would ask for such a large amount from them even if they do not have it. They will be more likely to contribute something if they cannot afford the maximum amount. Yet, if all you do is ask for the maximum amount the contributors will feel it is all or nothing. So, give donors lower amount options.

30.WEBSITE FUNDRAISING

You must give people the option to contribute money through your website. This is a great way for people interested in your campaign to give and give more than once.

The Internet is a great place to get your message out, and to refer those interested in you to visit.

Your site needs to be secure. And, it must comply with the same election laws that govern your printed materials. Your treasurer should be directly involved in the development of the site in regards to collecting contributions. And your treasurer needs to make sure only legal donors are contributing, and if not, that your campaign quickly returns the money.

The look of the website should be consistent with your message. A good practice is to add your photos, videos, commercials (audio or video), calendar, press releases, and platform to the website before you unveil it to any other medium. This strategy is a tease, creating greater interest.

31 . CAUCUS

Partisan elections are the most involved of elections because of the number of steps involved to advance as a candidate. Unenrolled candidates have it much easier; they just file their certified petitions, and they might face a primary for a municipal election, but for them, it is mostly straight on to the general election.

Partisan elections after the petitions have been filed then move to a caucus phase or election of delegates to the state convention phase. The delegates at the party's state convention or the caucuses at the party's town or city committees vote on a slate of candidates for various offices, and usually on one candidate per office. The rules per state party vary dramatically, which is why it is important to understand the campaign schedule for your particular party. As I mentioned before, you do this during the research phase of the campaign.

After the caucus phase or delegate phase comes the convention, then after the convention comes the primary election, and the general election. For each phase, your strategy is the same. You focus on the voters who hold your election future in their hands.

During the caucus phase, you would visit with the voters who will elect the delegates to the state convention. Attend their town meetings, meet them at their homes or places of business, and ask them to select a delegate who supports you. During your research with party insiders, the insiders will enlighten you to this delicate and complicated process. Delegates are often elected officials or executive board members of the town or city partisan committee. It is not necessary to strong-arm the committees to get voters who support you elected as delegates; this can stir resentment and hurt people's feelings.

BEWARE!!

There is a thin line between aggressive campaigning and being down-right nasty. Politics is about being organized, diplomatic, and open to negotiation. Candidates come and go. Party insiders are just that: insiders. They will be with the party before and after your candidacy, so they deserve a great deal of respect and recognition. Bombing their committee with new people or trying to force your way into their good graces will not work. It will just cause a great deal of resentment, which could derail your campaign. Negotiate with party insiders for delegate support. Find out what they want and try to strike a deal. This makes them important and creates allies.

State conventions are mostly a shell of their former selves. Their outcomes are not usually binding. But, they do influence perception. The winners at the convention will get the press' attention. The losers are not completely out of the race. Most states allow the losers to continue on to the primary election. Yet, winning at the convention is a big boost to your viability as a candidate. The strategy is the same as the caucus: meet with each delegate who controls your fate at the convention, and make a good impression—give them a great reason to vote for you. Ask them to vote for you. Attend the convention. Meet with the delegates again and try to get to some of the parties and events to mingle even if you are the only candidate. The face-time is crucial for support.

The primary election is after the convention phase of the campaign of the respective party. This is your first attempt to meet voters and win their support. Up until now, all of your fundraising efforts will go toward influencing these voters.

TIP!!

Specific voters vote in partisan primary elections. These voters will appear on what is called a purged list. This purged list is the list of voters who have voted in a prior primary election for your party. Get the most recent purged list from the town or city clerk. If your district covers more than one town or city you will get those lists, too. Some districts cover towns and city precincts; you want the purge lists for each voting location of your district for the most recent primary. Usually, the purged list is in electronic form, which can be merged to create mailing lists, fundraising lists, phone calling lists, or polls.

You want to contact everyone on the purge list personally as the candidate, even if you are unopposed in the primary. The larger your district, the more distant you will be from your targeted voter in a personal way. Media ads and mailings can help make your appeal more personal in a large district. Town hall meetings can help make that personal appeal, too; they allow the voter a chance to be part of your candidacy. Even if the voter chooses not to attend the meeting, he or she makes an active decision not to participate. This is actually more personal than advertisements. Yet, even if you are running for office in a large district, personally meeting with voters goes a long way. Obviously, you cannot meet with everyone, but you should meet with as many as possible, even if you are the only primary candidate. If they feel you do not care to meet them, voters can be unforgiving. Don't make that mistake. The voters are everything.

Smaller district races require you to meet almost all the primary voters who form your base vote. If these people vote for you once, they will vote for you forever; they are extremely loyal. Some of these voters contribute to your campaign or become volunteers. If you spurn them, you sink yourself. If you meet them and they join your team, they will go the extra mile for you. The campaign will begin to take on a life of its own. A gauge of your popularity with voters are their letters to the editor in local papers. Another great sign of the validity of your candidacy is if your base voters write letters on your behalf without your persuasion. Also, radio talk show callers and guests on community television who say positive things about you are crucial measures of your campaign's efforts. Even if the dialogue is not positive, it shows your campaign influences voters' opinions.

BEWARE ! !

Planting letters to the editor, talk show call-ins, and hecklers at an opponent's event can be costly. Voters hate a candidate who seems conniving; they feel manipulated, and you will lose their hard to earn trust. It is much better to play off your supporters' genuine enthusiasm for you and your campaign. Support their initiative to hold campaign signs at an opponent's rally. Support their letters, call-ins, and appearances as long as it is in-line with your message. The genuineness will shine through even if your opponent is screaming about how deceptive you are. Your supporters will actually fight for you.

Be careful not to support criminal activity at the hands of your supporters. Taking down an opponent's lawn sign, pushing or verbally assaulting your opponent's supporters, peeling off the opponent's bumper stickers and the like shows that you are fine with being a thug. Voters do not like conniving and they do not like intimidation. There is a fine line between taking an aggressive stand for a candidate and being a hoodlum. Once a supporter crosses that line, the campaign and the candidate either should denounce the action and the individual or reel them in quickly before they cause more damage. If a supporter commits a criminal offense, let the appropriate authorities know: be proactive and be responsible.

32.ADVERTISING

Whether or not you have an opponent, you should spend the bulk of your fundraising on advertising for the primary election. It takes time for most voters to become familiar with you. Nothing can reinforce your name better than meeting the voter personally. Next to a face-to-face meeting, the following advertising media carry the greatest impact from the greatest impact to the least:

- Television
- Internet (website and video)
- Radio
- Phone calls
- Billboards
- Newspapers (tombstones)
- Yard signs
- Bumper stickers
- Miscellaneous

Your goal is to raise money to cover all of these media. Television remains the most powerful, and should be where you will spend the most money and time on your advertising. Your website would is next; it is a vital part of the campaign but it does not reach and affect voters as much as television does. The latter media are not as persuasive by themselves as television, but coupled with television advertising voters can find them incredibly memorable.

Television displays a marvelous phenomenon. As a culture, we accept what we see on television personally. We identify with and are motivated by characters and personalities. So, a candidate has an excellent opportunity to connect with voters often more intimately than in-person. A face-to-face meeting will always be the best way to win votes, especially as you remember to ask people for their votes. Yet, television advertising can come very close.

33. TELEVISION ADVERTISING

Television advertising means advertising through cable, satellite, and network services. It does not include embedded video on a website. The advertising is called a "spot." The spot is either 30 or 60 seconds long. I am not going to belabor the details of a TV commercial. Hopefully, you know what one looks like, and if not, someone on your campaign should have seen one and can enlighten you on the context.

To be a successful candidate, you need a compelling TV advertising campaign. It is quite simple. The first commercial reveals your autobiography, the second commercial features your main issue, and the third commercial contains your "get out the vote" message.

Record all of the commercials with you, the candidate, delivering the messages. Each spot should be only 30 seconds. Your message should include an introduction, then the main point, and finally, ask for the vote, with the legal disclaimer at the end.

When you think of TV political advertising, presidential campaigns often come to mind. Presidential campaigns focus mainly on this form of advertising. Such candidates have big budgets and a number of advertising professionals at their disposal. They can create several TV commercials in a short time frame, which is not usually a luxury candidates running for other offices have, nor does it have to be.

TV advertising is surprisingly less expensive than you might think, and with cable operators you can beam your message right at the voter you are trying to persuade to vote for you. You need only a minimum of the three television advertisements illustrated. Can you add more? Sure.

Cable networks and your local cable operator can offer the most cost-effective way to target your voters and broadcast your message. Also, your local cable operator can be a good source for shooting and producing the spot in an economical way. Satellite networks and major networks can be more expensive and less focused. Major network advertising can snag a wider audience for greater popularity, but cable networks, especially the news networks, are capable of reaching the right people who can vote for you in the primary or general election.

Cable networks allow you to adjust your voting population for your primary election or your general election. Your local cable provider has a large amount of data about their viewers you can cross-reference with the voters you think will most likely vote for you. Then, they will match the network(s) that will best reach those households for your success in getting your message to them. You might need multiple networks, and your channels can change as the focus of your campaign shifts from the primary to the general election.

The context of the advertisement is the same as it would be if you met the voter in-person. It is you, the candidate, speaking into the camera to the voter, delivering your message and asking for his or her vote.

BEWARE ! !

There is no need for gimmicks, animation, or other attention-getting strategies. It is you directly asking voters for their votes, to persuade them to vote for you. This approach is best, and it is less expensive.

Music and effects can easily distract and confuse voters. People could remember your jingle, but forget your request for their votes. Be perfectly clear and direct. Leave no room for interpretation.

34. TV ADVERTISING CALENDAR

For best results, start TV advertising eight weeks before the primary or general election. You should run your autobiography advertisement for two weeks, then take a week off. This is called a pulse. Then pulse for two weeks with your main issue, and stop for one week. Lastly, pulse for two weeks, plus the days leading up and including Election Day of the Get out the Vote (GOTV) advertisement.

Depending on the type of election, primary or general, keep in mind the audience you are trying to reach will change. Do not assume voters are paying attention to your campaign all the time. So, if you air your autobiography advertisement again after you just broadcast it in the primary election, it will not hurt you for the general election; it will actually help you, as it will let you get acquainted with voters who have not met you. This is the same for the other pulses.

35. ENTER THE CELEBRITY

You will know when your advertising and hard work pays off when voters recognize you and you do not recognize them. And, when you get considered or treated like a celebrity. (Most of the time, when people complain about your ads and seeing them too much, they are not voters.)

The celebrity phenomenon shows an interesting effect of campaigning. It is seen mostly with candidates who do television advertising. Viewers will begin to treat you like a celebrity; this usually means awkward introductions, requests for autographs, and for photos with them, which is good.

When people notice you on the street and make a big deal about it, it can be unsettling at first. After a while it can become addictive, and that can be dangerous. Keep your candidacy in perspective. Your candidacy is one of many and it has a brief lifespan. After the election, the world will move on. So, you have to make a positive and memorable impact during this short span. Any type of grandstanding or shameless popularity stunts will backfire almost immediately. Let your message speak for you and stay on script. Your popularity will ebb and flow. The only important factor is the outcome of the election: you win.

36. GOING NEGATIVE

Negative campaigning is volatile, but an effective practice. Anytime you disagree with your opponent and mention it publicly you are "going negative." It is unavoidable. You cannot be successful and hope to win if you do not contrast yourself from your opponent. You do not need to be nasty. You do not have to sensationalize your differences. You should state why voters should hire you instead of anyone else.

TV advertising is a popular medium for negative campaigning. Political pundits and the press in presidential campaigns mostly talk about it. For negative campaigning to work, voters should be familiar with you as a candidate and think positively enough of you to dislike and vote against the opponent with the new or reinforced negative information the voters already know. If you dislike something about your opponent, say it and make sure it is in your advertising—this should already be part of your message, anyway.

BEWARE!!

Negative campaigning can be taken to an extreme. Personal attacks can damage you more than your opponent. It can look desperate and angry, two traits voters dislike. Leave it to the press to dig up the personal dirt. Stay above the fray, even if your opponent's behavior has been criminal. The press will do all the work for you if your opponent has been less than a model citizen. Stick to your message on how you will be better than your opponent once elected.

37. POLLING

Polling is an important tool to measure voters' feedback. As soon as you advance from the state convention, start polling. Volunteers can easily conduct polls. Or, you can hire a polling firm, and in some cases, colleges or universities will conduct polling on your behalf. You can use volunteers to call potential voters you have determined from your research are most likely to vote for you. The trick to good polling is to identify a good sample. Samples can be conducted on four basic age groups and be quite revealing. The age groups are, with their overall (interest):

- 18-25 (starting out)
- 26-35 (getting established)
- 35-55 (family)
- 55+ (retirement)

Usually, you just need to contact about 10 percent of your specific age group. An easy way to tell their ages is by their addresses. Where they live is a good indicator of who they are and what matters to them. The streets on your purged voter list identify the neighborhoods and they reveal a lot about the character and the ages of people who live in them.

Gender, race, and religion are important variables, but are often not as important to elections as you might believe. Most people have a lot in common and are concerned about the same things. They also vote similarly. That is why you can take a 10 percent sample and ask them their opinion of you and come almost as close as if you polled all of them.

Your volunteers can call or visit these voters and simply ask two questions about voting for you or for your opponent. When you get the results, you can see which age group is leaning your way and which one is not. And, from the data you can adjust your campaign to reach out to the voters.

Example: the 55+ group is not with you, but more than half of the 25 to 35 age group sampled are voting for you. You would then focus on personal contact and TV advertising for the 55+ group, and spend less time with the 25 to 35 group, but do not ignore them.

Often the argument will be if the 55+ group is not with you, you should focus on another group that is with you, such as the 25 to 35 group, to compensate for the other group's deficiency. That is true only IF you know the 55+ hates you. If not, you can win them over by personally visiting them. The 55+ group really likes personal interaction with candidates and can be persuaded to vote for you if you ask them face-to-face. Ignore them, and out of spite the 55+ group will vote for your opponent.

The older the voter demographic, the more interested and involved they will be in the political process and in your candidacy, but they are not likely as interested in working for your campaign. The younger the voter, the less likely he or she will be interested in your candidacy, but if they are interested, they tend to be good workers. So, structure your advertising accordingly to reap the greatest rewards for your advertising dollars for voter penetration and workers.

38.VOLUNTEER VS. PROFESSIONAL

When you advertise heavily, your campaign is considered to be professional. When you use a lot of people to spread your word it is considered a volunteer campaign. Most campaigns are a mixture of both professional and volunteer labor. But to have the best chance to win, focus on a professional campaign.

If you look at your campaign in the voters' eyes, your view will be limited. Even presidential campaigns are not always on the collective minds of the voters, and they are the most popular of campaigns. So, your message should be targeted to voters who will most likely vote for you often, and when they are receptive to it. Example: it is much better to see your ad on a news network than to see a few supporters holding your signs at a street intersection. The voter needs to be reminded often of your existence, especially as you get closer to the election date. The best way to do this is to have your TV advertisement invade voters' homes while they are watching their favorite programs. The voter associates your ad with what they watch. This gives you and your campaign greater legitimacy and celebrity status.

39.ABSENTEE BALLOTS

Absentee voting is becoming more popular. Absentee ballots are usually available well before Election Day. But, the ballots are not usually counted until after the primary or general election votes are cast and counted. During this period, it is important to maintain your polling and advertising. The advertising pulses will ensure your message is in front of these early voters. Many of these voters are in the military. Your city or town clerk can tell you who actually requested an absentee ballot. The best practice would be to visit that voter and ask for his or her vote—if not in-person, at least with a phone call. But, a visit is more compelling.

40.GET OUT THE VOTE

Your "get out the vote" drive starts three weeks before the election and builds to Election Day. You hear the political media talk about undecided voters, partisan voters, or independents. As a candidate, you should assume all voters are undecided. Most voters will begin to make a decision about who they are going to vote for three weeks before the election.

This means the bulk of your advertising should be spent in this time period. If you are a candidate with a small account balance from fundraising, this is when you are going to spend it to the get the greatest "bang for your buck." Three days before the election, your advertising and polling should accelerate, and your advertising should stop on Election Day. You should spend the three days before election day with your phone bank calling voters to vote for you based on your polling results, focusing on the voters who are still undecided.

Most voters will remain undecided until they fill-out their ballots. For voters, this is a vulnerable time. So, your name and message must linger in their minds. This is where the three weeks of advertising and last three days of phone calls will be powerful for connecting with voters in the voting booth. So, your advertising needs to continue, and through Election Day.

In the real world of campaigning, all voters are undecided. Think about when you vote: do you leave yourself a little bit of doubt just in case one of the candidates self-destructs at the last second? Of course you do. Even the most partisan voter still proceeds to the ballot with a degree of caution. That is why it is so important to maintain a constant advertising presence the last three weeks of the campaign. Your constant message will help alleviate voters' anxiety, and keep your candidacy on their minds.

BEWARE ! !

The question often arises, why not just spend all of your money and advertise the last three days of the election? Remember where you started. You started as an unknown and rose to become a political celebrity. You need to develop a relationship with voters to get them to vote for you. This takes time, and you can't accomplish it in just three days. Your candidacy requires a vigilant effort to send your message throughout the election year. The last three weeks of the campaign allow you to reinforce a memorable message in the voting booth. What you do not want to have happen is for the voter to see your name on the ballot and say,"Oh yeah, whatever happened that person? I have not heard of them lately." This internal conversation will be a vote for your opponent.

41. POLL CHECK

During your three weeks of intense polling and advertising, you need your campaign to organize a poll check team. For every polling location in your district, you need two paid or volunteer staff members to sit at the polls on Election Day and check voters' names as they arrive to vote. The primary reason for this is to give the phone bank a running account of who is and is not coming in to vote. The phone bank can then shift their calls to those who do not seem to be voting and persuade them to go to the polls and vote for you.

The other role the poll check team plays is to ensure the polls are being run according to the law. For example, a poll could open late, a ballot box could break and the municipality might need to open it up or remove it, arguments could erupt, voters might not follow designated routes to polling locations, voters could loiter in the polling location, the opponent's people could be inside a restricted space at the polling location, or the tally of the votes after the polls close might not be done legitimately. If anything seems contrary to the integrity of the voting process, the team should call the team leader, not you, the candidate. The team leader then rehearses the event with you while you are calling voters. The two of you decide how to resolve the alleged grievance.

The secretary of state or the town or city clerk will have a rulebook on how election ballots are to be collected. Every team member should have a copy of these rules. So it would be prudent to make sure that your team members will have the courage to report and intervene if there is an infraction. The rulebook will specify how the polling locations are to operate and what to do to if a violation occurs. The team leader needs to follow these rules and report punctually. You have only the day of the election to contest any discrepancies.

Make sure your team has all of the lists of voters for their polling locations. Your team will need pencils and rulers to cross-out names, and it is helpful for each teammate to have cellphones programmed with everyone's numbers for an easier information flow.

42 . PHONE BANK

The phone bank is the last three days before the election and Election Day. During the three weeks of intense advertising, you will also organize your phone bank. From your polling data, select the voters they should target and call them. The bulk of your volunteers need to be up for this effort. And with that in mind, they should be prepared and participate in some simulation training so their conversations flow smoothly, and to reduce any anxiety well ahead of time.

The phone bank will require many phones and phone lines. It works best when the phone bank is in an office, not in volunteers' homes. Keep plenty of food and water around for frequent breaks, but at the same time try to limit distractions. The phone lines should be installed well in advance. The simulation drills will also help ensure the phones and the lines work fine.

43. ELECTION DAY

The first order of business is for you and your staff to vote at the polls as soon as they open. To get a photo and an interview, the press might want to know when you are going to vote, so inform them the day before about when and where you are going to be. Your poll checkers should vote first, and then the rest of your campaign, including yourself. Your poll checkers will then start checking in voters and maintaining a critical eye on the polling location.

You would then visit each polling location to shake a few hands with voters and supporters. You should be firing up the phone bank and getting the vote to the polls one hour after the polls open. At this time, you will be leading the charge and making calls at the phone bank. The phone bank keeps working until a half hour before the polls close. Now, you are preparing to attend your election night event.

Your volunteers will want to do a bunch of things. Let your campaign manager or leader handle them. And be as liberal with the volunteers' support as the money will allow. If the volunteers want to hold signs, pass out donuts, or hand out push pieces door-to-door, let them. The bulk of your volunteers and staff should be on the phones, though. The phone bank is vital, and could make the difference between a win and a loss.

44. ELECTION NIGHT

Win or lose, the press will want your response. It is a good idea to hold an election night party—win or lose—to thank your supporters. Inform the press where the party will be held, and give them your cellphone number so they can interview you. During this chat, be gracious and polite. No matter the outcome, now is not the time to attack your opponent. It is onward and upward.

If you win, explain to the press how grateful you are for the voters and for their trust, and that you will begin to push your platform as soon as you are sworn-in. If you lose, thoroughly thank all of your supporters and leave the door open for another campaign.

45. WRAPPING UP

After the election, nothing turns people off more than seeing leftover campaign debris. This is the time to clean out offices, pick up yard signs, remove banners, billboards, and other advertising. Before the election is over, line-up your volunteers for this task, because they might not stay committed afterward. Voters will remember the candidate who left a mess behind, as will the towns in your district. Be professional and clean it up.

46. TRANSITION

You are a winner. Congratulations! Now put your transition team to work and prepare the new office for your first day on the job. Start with getting in touch with the administrator over the office in which you have been elected. For legislators, as an example, you would inquire with the secretary of state to see what the legal protocols are for transition. Just like on your campaign, there is a timetable for certain legal matters to take place before being sworn-in, and then you are sworn-in. In the meantime, have your transition team contact the current elected official and see what your team can do to transition as smoothly as possible.

You can form your transition team from key members of your campaign staff. You might want to retain some of the current official's staff. You can perform a lot of political maneuvering to achieve success the first day in office. So you can build on the planks in your platform, you might want to reach out to a trusted mentor you met along the campaign trail. Yet, campaigning and public service are two different

animals. And successful public service is not the scope of this book.

47.WERE YOU A SUCCESSFUL CANDIDATE?

T he fact that you ran for office is courageous and needs to be applauded, no matter the outcome. There are no magic formulas for winning elections. Unless you control the ballot box, you cannot guarantee an election. What you can measure is the electorate's response to you and your campaign; this obviously comes in the form of a win or loss, but also in the political celebrity status you achieved.

The political celebrity is your status of success. If you won, you can build on your celebrity and stay in that office for life or seek higher office. Yet, a loss is not the end of the world. And, a loss will be more than likely the outcome for a first time-candidate.

You will be amazed at how many doors of opportunity can open for you from a political contest due to your celebrity, even if you did not win. Take a look at these opportunities and weigh them carefully. See if they increase the quality of your life and those you love. But, do not be afraid to run again if necessary. The rule of thumb is three campaigns to actually win that specific office. So, look at a loss as a milestone, not a failure. It can take a while to gain the trust of the electorate, but this method quickly shortens the timeframe. Yet again, it can take a couple of campaigns to modify your message and for the electorate to embrace you before you win the office you seek.

If you achieved 30 percent of the vote or better in the primary or general election you are considered a viable candidate for a future election. Obviously, the closer you get to winning, the more viable you will seem to your supporters the next time. Your ability to raise money throughout the campaign will be another indicator of your viability, but that shows in your overall percentage of the vote.

BEWARE!!

After a loss, your critics will say you spent your time and money in the wrong places, plus you did not raise enough money to win. For pundits and political operatives who work for a specific party, this is a default position. Partisan leadership does not take the blame for their party's wins and losses. It is always the inferior candidate's fault. Be prepared for this, but DO NOT retaliate. A public fight inside the party will not help you. ALWAYS speak highly and positively of those who supported you, even if they are trashing you in the press.

Do not believe your critics, either. They are not to be trusted because they are not giving advice and did not participate in the campaign. They have their own agendas, especially if they are being paid for their opinions. The truth of your success lies in the number of voters who voted for you. We have to assume the ballot box contains legitimate ballots and what the ballots show is how to measure your success. Your critics will never know the minds of the voters—they are guessing, so do not take it to heart. And again, do not retaliate.

48. THE DAY AFTER

If you have lost the election, the following day can be one of the most depressing days of your life. You have dropped yourself and your loved ones into the political shark tank. You have had your character attacked, lied about, and threatened, and have spent a lot of money hoping for a more positive outcome. BUT, by the third day after the election, you are ready to run for office again.

This manic-depressive phase is natural and necessary. Other than a military campaign, a political campaign is a true life-and-death struggle. Religion, war, and politics are kissing cousins that share the same intensity and respect. Politics is filled with problems to remedy. And serious candidates need to be emboldened to solve serious life or death issues for the betterment of our human family. So, it is natural to feel the weight of the campaign and after it is over, sit in a dark room to decompress. Yet, it will pass and your desire will return as if you had not lost.

BEWARE ! !

It is not uncommon for successful political candidates to get the bug and become junkies looking for a political fix wherever they can find it.

Campaigning for office is a rite of passage. It puts you ahead of all those who do not have the courage to make a difference. But, in the same breath, you are a leader and are ethically sworn to protect those who cannot protect themselves. Do not use your newfound political skills for diabolical purposes. Criminal activity is not right. Crime is not OK at any price. Control your political appetite; travel on lighted highways and do not drive down dark roads. Keep the faith in making the world a better place through your selfless leadership, and stay away from the selfish tendency to just get yours and the heck with everyone else.

49.MOVING FORWARD

The political process is fascinating and complex. It has been a pleasure to share with you the inner workings of campaigning so you can be a successful candidate. If you have not decided to run for office, try working on a campaign as a volunteer. Take notes. Compare what that campaign is doing to what I have offered here. See what worked for them and what did not. Yet, at some point, jump into the ring. It will be worth it.

.

Dale Fegel Jr.

ABOUT THE AUTHOR

Dale Leslie Fegel Jr. was born and raised in the conservative mecca of western Michigan where he developed a love for the election process.

That passion for politics grew in the decidedly Democratic bastion of New England where he ran for office and managed the campaigns of several other Republicans, Democrats and Independent candidates for local, state and federal offices.

Dale has done graduate work at Suffolk University in Political Science with an emphasis on campaigns, had his own local political program on NPR, and served as the alternate delegate for Massachusetts at the Republican convention in 2000—the year he helped run Sen. John McCain's presidential campaign efforts in Massachusetts.

Dale currently lives in Maine with his wife and three children where he is active in the community and Republican politics. He maintains a blog on politics and the political process at www.dalefegeljr.com.

One thing more...

I f you want a no-nonsense, concise guide to help you be a better leader at work, at home, on the playing field or in your community, this is the book you've been looking for! If, on the other hand, you just want to sit on the sidelines and watch the world pass you by, then do NOT pick up this book. It is definitely not for you.

If you want to make a difference in this world, but you don't know where to start. Start with "Leadership: A Full Contact Sport." Dale Fegel Jr. gives you leadership training like you've never seen before. It is pure guidance based on real-world experiences that worked. He gives it to you straight in a way that will beat you up and leave you begging for more.

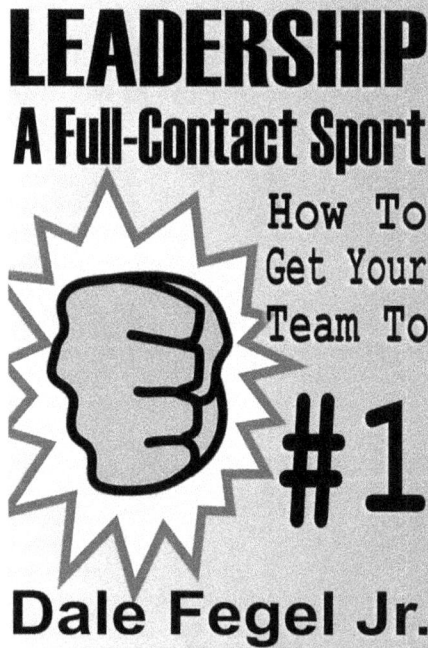

Get it now only on Amazon for Kindle!!